Encyclopedia of Positive Questions

Volume One

Using Appreciative Inquiry To Bring Out The Best In Your Organization

Diana Whitney
David L. Cooperrider
Amanda Trosten-Bloom
Brian S. Kaplin

Published by: *Lakeshore Communications*
24100 Lakeshore Blvd.
Euclid, OH 44123
(216) 731-0234

Printed in the United States of America
C D E F G
ISBN 1893435-334

This publication is designed to provide accurate and authoritative information with regard to the subject matter involved. It is sold with the understanding that the publisher is not engaged in rendering legal, accounting or other professional advice. If legal advice or other expert assistance is required, the services of a qualified professional person should be sought.

-From: **A Declaration of Principles**, jointly adopted by a Committee of the American Bar Association and a Committee of Publishers and Associations.

Visit our home page at: http://www.lakeshorepublishers.com

Acknowledgements

This book was originally published for the employees of the former GTE, now Verizon. It would not be possible without the collaboration of Jean Moore, Dan Young, Maureen Garrison, Geri England and Gary Kebschuell. They were our clients and thinking partners for over four years, while we introduced Appreciative Inquiry to the people of GTE. It was an exciting time for all of us. Together we created many innovative, first-time, applications for Appreciative Inquiry. As a result, GTE won the ASTD Award for Best Culture Change Initiative in 1997. It is a credit to the extraordinary commitment, caring and creativity of these leaders of change.

Encyclopedia of Positive Questions

Table of Contents

Introduction

In a very real sense most human searches are a success. Not only
do we seem to find whatever it is we are looking for but, as the
legendary CEO Sam Walton demonstrated, when we search the
world around us for what is best about a human system, the
positive qualities tend to multiply. The active surfacing of good
news—of opportunities, strengths, achievements, visions,
innovations and the like—is not an avoidance of reality; it is the
best way to improve reality.

The practice of asking positive questions not only brings out the
best in people and organizations, it also amplifies and magnifies
the most positive life giving possibilities for the future.

But before getting too far into this book put the idea to a simple
test. Next time, before a team meeting begins, ask people to turn
quickly to the person next to them and share stories from their
experience. Put the following positive question up on a flipchart
for everyone to see, and ask each person to "interview" their
partner for ten minutes. Instruct people to discover as much from
their partner as they can by asking the following question:

*Reflecting back on your entire career think about the most
memorable **team experience** you have ever had...a high-point
when you felt really effective, energized, and proud...Tell me the*

story... about the time when you were part of a really great team? What made the team a success? What was it about you that helped make it great? What did you learn then that can help us be a great team now?

Watch what happens to the energy in the room! After this mini "appreciative inquiry" ask people how it went. Ask people to share an adjective or a phrase that describes their experience of the interview. Here is what you will likely hear:

- It was inspiring;
- We needed much more time;
- We connected deeply;
- I learned what truly matters to my friend;
- It was refreshing and mind expanding;
- It was filled with surprises;
- It was entertaining;
- It was informative;
- We shared a common dream;
- It felt safe.

This booklet, filled with dozens of questions just like this, on everything from business strategy to empowerment, can decisively bring about a more positive world – both in our organizations and personal lives. Put simply, the message of this powerful resource is this: *it is the questions that count. The questions we ask do make a difference.*

People Live in the Worlds Their Questions Create

From childhood on some of us seem to be braced for disappointment. And when we are, we then find disappointments in abundance. Life becomes a story of broken dreams and disillusion. Our heroes always seem to collapse. What can go wrong seems always to go wrong. Our questions, even when well intentioned, become increasingly negative. *How can I escape this unhappiness? I wonder what the children will do wrong today? Why is the morale so low in this company? How did we lose market share so quickly? Why can't I do anything right?*

Others of us, however, are guided by a different search. We seem to be moving along the high road. The scenery inspires, and the people along the way are very helpful. We seem to be surrounded by goodness and good fortune. Our question seems to be of a different nature and more positive. *What is it that we might do together that we can't do alone? How can I bring out the best in my children? What is about her that is so inspiring? What is my calling?*

Research shows one common denominator.[1] After interviewing 100 of the most successful and happy people they could find, researchers were confused in the beginning. At first blush, there was nothing in common—certainly not education or socio-economic background. Some were grade school dropouts but had great careers in business, while others had received doctorate degrees. Some had come from wealth while others had risen above the poverty into which they were born, some were high-level executives while others were front line workers and secretaries. Of

---

[1] See the research reported in chapter six, <u>Happiness is an Inside Job</u> by John Powell.

all the categories, the nearest thing to a common denominator was that a slight majority came from small towns of under 15,000 people. However, in the final tally of all the information, a clear pattern did emerge and the search was rewarded with success. The research found that each and every one of the 100 people had a special capability – *"to look for and find what is good in him or her self, in others, and in all the situations of life."*

The word "goodfinder" had to be invented to describe this common trait. Because of their never-ending search for the positive, the good, the better, and the possible—and because of the ability to see and amplify the best in people and situations around them—these leaders were successful. People wanted to be around them. Those same people felt valued and understood. Strengths were elevated. Weaknesses became irrelevant. And nothing about the leadership was Pollyannaish; the goodfinders had examples, hard data, and stories from everywhere of golden innovations, achievements, capabilities, opportunities and the like. They were experts at deliberately noticing, anticipating, and magnifying positive potential. And for our purposes here, one lesson stands out above all others:

If you truly wish to change your world, you must change your way of asking questions. It could be that the moment you do so, a totally different world will take shape around you.

The Idea of Positive Change

One of the CEO's who tested many of the questions outlined herein confided: "this handbook on the power of positive questions has implications for *every* aspect of our business: measurement systems, customer focus groups, quality management, teambuilding, performance appraisal, surveys, indeed, everything where we ask questions or gather data. But the importance of this approach goes beyond business ... (pause)... I only wish I had the benefit of these ideas a few short years ago when my children were growing up."

This practical handbook has forty questions that can transform your approach to leadership and organizational development. Not one of the questions has the word "problem" in it. Indeed, the only thing the questions are meant to do is help people discover strengths, assets, and best practices. And this is deliberate. Put simply, the message of this resource is this: positive results will suddenly appear for you virtually everywhere the more you are able to see the best in others (your children, colleagues, partners, competitors), see the best in yourself, and then ask questions that bring out and amplify the best in your organization.

This book of questions is not about more knowledge, but new knowing. It is an invitation to join a positive revolution. It is about a methodology that is re-shaping the way organizations all over the world are thinking about change. It is an approach to leadership called *Appreciative Inquiry (AI)*.

The first section of this booklet lists eleven ways to use positive questions for bringing out the best in your organization. The ideas are loosely presented. It is up to you to tighten them up to fit your purposes. Review this section and then review the sample questions in the second section. They are only sample questions, intended for you to modify to fit the situations you manage. This booklet is intended to give you ideas. It is not designed to give you a step-by-step formula for using positive questions. As you know, leadership is an art and not a science. Keep in mind that "words create worlds." Choose your questions wisely and intentionally. What you ask determines what you find. And what you find sets the agenda for action in your organization.

Section three lists ten ways to use success stories and to spread best practices throughout your organization. Knowledge management is key to competitive advantage in today's fast-changing business environment. Being able to learn from the best, within your organization; and to quickly and widely provide access to lessons learned, creates a unique work environment and competitive advantage.

Should you want to go beyond the use of these sample questions and create your own questions and <u>Appreciative Interview Guide</u>, section four provides information on how to choose topics. Section five gives guidelines for writing positive questions. Section six shows you how to pull it all together into a coherent interview guide. Section seven and eight then provide you with sample interview guides.

SECTION 1

Eleven Ways to Use Positive Questions

Your day as a manager is full of opportunities.Whether you manage people or projects, the work you do gets done through communication, through the interactions and conversations you have with people. The questions in this book are intended to help you focus communication on the positive possibilities. The following eleven ways to use positive questions come from the experience of managers in organizations around the world.

1. **Get Staff Meetings Off to a Good Start** – The way meetings begin most often sets the tone for how they will proceed and what will be accomplished. Select one of the positive questions in this booklet or make up one of your own related to a current business issue. Begin your next staff meeting with a round table discussion. Ask everyone to share answers to the question. After the sharing is complete, ask people to reflect on what they heard and learned in the process. Starting meetings with stories of success and accomplishment will set a tone for further success during your time together.

2. **Coach for High Performance** – When people are reminded of their capabilities and strengths they are more likely to build upon them. All too often coaching is focused on what's gone wrong and what needs to improve. Helping people recall their high performance patterns (the habits, relationships and situations that contribute to their success) and feel a sense of self-confidence is a great way to enhance high performance. Choose 2-3 of the positive questions in this booklet and use

them to begin your next coaching session. Listen carefully during the interview to identify the habits, relationships and situations that contribute to your interviewee's success. After the interview reflect back what you heard from your interviewee about her or his high performance pattern. Ask your partner how these success patterns can be applied to the current situation, to bring out her or his best performance.

3. **Transform "Problem Talk" to "Possibility Talk"** — Problem talk leads to problem thinking and acting; it includes conversations about who or what caused the problem and therefore, is to blame. More time is spent looking backward, trying to understand the problem, than looking forward to explore positive possibilities. Conversations can be turned around with the use of a positive question. The questions in this booklet can be used to transform difficult conversations. Try using a positive question the next time an employee or colleague comes to you complaining about a problem. Listen for awhile and then ask one of the questions in this booklet (make certain that it is relevant to the issue being discussed). For example, if a colleague complains about lack of cooperation from another person or group, you might ask the positive question about teamwork, cooperation or even shared vision, to turn the conversation toward positive possibilities.

4. **Create Dialogue to Foster Shared Meaning** – People work better together and achieve more when they are aligned around a shared purpose, values and goals. Shared meaning leads to cooperative action, mutual understanding and respect. Next time you are with a group of people where open dialogue and shared meaning needs to occur, select 2–3 questions from this booklet and ask them to interview one another. Allow about 15 minutes for each interview. After the interviews

have group members share what they learned. This is especially effective as an opening to a discussion of sensitive issues.

5. **Demonstrate Positive Intent and Trust with Customers**
Exceptional customer relations depend on positive intent and trust. It is often difficult to assume that the customer is always right when face-to-face with an angry or frustrated customer. The use of a positive question, in the midst of customer frustration, demonstrates a willingness to go forward together based on what works for the customer and the company. Try it. After listening to a customer's frustration, ask a positive question and see what happens. There are several appropriate questions to choose from in this booklet. Select the one or two which make the most sense to you, keep them in your hip pocket, and draw on them when the tension runs high. Watch what happens.

6. **Create a Learning Organization** – Perhaps the most exciting outcome of managing with positive questions is the tremendous learning that occurs for you and the people you interview. The winning organizations of the next decade will be those with the greatest capacity for learning. Inquiry based on positive questions (what is called Appreciative Inquiry) can help you as build a learning organization. Select two to three of the questions in this booklet and interview five to eight people. Keep track of the patterns and themes that you hear and the most exciting best practices. After you finish your interviews get a group together to share what you learned. Encourage them to conduct interviews and then to meet, in person or on-line, to share what they learned.

7. **Build High Performance Teams** – When teamwork is

important, people need to get to know one another –their values, their personal aspirations and especially how they work when at their best. You can foster teamwork by selecting 2 – 3 of the positive questions in this booklet and asking team members to share their answers out loud with one another. Take time for each person to reflect on what matters to them at work, and to share their story with the team. After everyone has shared, ask the group to identify common themes, or to list all the resources the members of the team collectively bring to the team's endeavors.

8. **Conduct Project Reviews that Make a Difference** – All too often a project ends in silence and project members go on to the next big challenge. Taking time to celebrate and to learn from work well-done keeps both enthusiasm and achievement flowing. All projects have their own personalities, their ups and downs, their highpoints and their memorable moments. Use 2 – 3 of the questions in this book to learn about the memorable moments of a recent project and to identify key success factors. You might gather the project team and answer the questions together; or you might interview team members and project stakeholders and share your findings with team members. Whatever you do, use it as a time to recognize and celebrate the job well-done, as well as to cull out lessons for the future. Positive projection and reviews can give people energy and ideas for the work ahead.

9. **Build Self-Esteem** – In all of us there is latent power – strengths and capacities that are unrecognized and under-utilized. By asking positive questions you can help another person recognize and own their own positive potential. In this way you can help draw out and build self-esteem. You might try this with an employee, a friend or a child. Select an

appropriate set of questions from this booklet and set aside 45 minutes to one hour for a personal interview. Draw out experiences that help your interviewee reflect on highlights of her or his past and dreams for her or his future. Be sure to listen carefully and restate what you hear as the strengths and capabilities of your interviewee. After you share what you learned in the interview, ask your interviewee to share what he or she learned about his or herself.

10. **Plan a Course of Action for the Future** – Clarity and commitment to a course of future action can only be generated in conversation. Plans written by one person, alone at a computer, late at night do not instill commitment or ownership – no matter how well disseminated. Conversation leads to action. The next time you want to engage a group of people in planning for the future, start by asking a series of positive questions. The most compelling paths forward are built upon the successes of the past. Continuity enables change. Select 3 – 5 questions from this booklet and ask each person to interview one other person for at least 30 minutes each. After the interviews, bring the group together. Have the group share key points, common themes and core capabilities of the group. Use these discussions as a baseline for conversations about strategies, objectives and action plans for the future.

11. **Create Your Own Interview Guide** – Inquiry-rich learning organizations are uniquely poised for success in this new world of information and globalization. And a good way to develop a culture of inquiry is to make Appreciative Inquiry a way of life. Use the sample questions in this booklet – along with the guidelines provided in Sections 4-6 – as inspiration for creating systemic inquiries that are customized and unique to

your organization.

Choose 3-5 questions that are relevant and desirable to your organization's future and create your own interview guide. Get people involved in conducting interviews, sharing stories and lessons learned and envisioning positive possibilities for the future of your origination. Remember, the more you enjoy the process, the more positive the results will be.

SECTION 2

Sample Positive Questions

Questions are fateful. They create a conversational agenda, which in turn becomes the context for envisioning and enacting the future. Thus, the seeds of change are implicit in the first questions we ask. The more positive the question the more positive the potential for transformation.

Best-in-Class

Best-in-class means being as good as it gets – doing something better than anyone else who does the same thing. Organizations become best-in-class by identifying and nurturing best-in-class qualities within their departments, functions, and processes.

Best-in-class departments and functions demonstrate levels of operational excellence that are beyond the reach of other "good" organizations. The way they do things allows them to accomplish exceptional results, along with high levels of employee satisfaction.

1. What is it about you and the way you do your job that's best-in-class? What effect do these skills or behaviors have on you and your sense of self? What effect do they have on your co-workers? In your department? In the organization as a whole?

2. How about your function or department? What are the things that make this group the best that it can possibly be? Think

about addressing such things as your products, services, technology, processes, etc.

3. Put yourself in our customers' shoes. What do you think they would say if we asked them what makes this organization best-in-class?

4. Think of another business or company that you admire . . . one that you either know well or have heard of. It could be your corner grocery store, or an internationally recognized organization.

- What, in your experience, makes that organization best-in-class?
- What do they do that we could learn to do better?

Career Development

In today's rapidly-changing business environment, an organization's success depends on the learning capacity of its members. In successful organizations career development is a responsibility shared between the organization and its employees. Career coaching, training and opportunities for advancement demonstrate the organization's value for career development. When people are committed to career development, they are in a mode of continuous learning about their job and about themselves. They focus on their unique gifts and talents and their contribution to the organization. As people develop they have more to offer their team and the organization. Everyone benefits from learning.

1. Tell me about the most challenging and exciting career development opportunity you have experienced. What was it? Why did you decide on it? What made it challenging and exciting? How did you benefit? How did the organization benefit?

2. How do you learn best? Tell me about a time when you learned something very challenging. What contributed to your learning?

3. Tell me about the work experience in which you have learned the most. Tell me about the situation. Who else was involved and what did they do? What did you do to foster your own development? What made this a highpoint learning experience?

Can-Do Coaching

When organizations are at their best, people at all levels of the organization engage in can-do coaching with one another. Supervisors who see their team members through the lens of an appreciative eye build human capacity and team capacity at the same time. Can-do coaching empowers people by showing them when they are on the right track. It also allows them freedom and encourages them to think for themselves. Can-do coaching helps people discover their own abilities. With the support that positive coaching provides, people find they can do amazing things. Coaching provides a unique opportunity to instill a can-do attitude. By coaching each other, we build relationships and capacities.

1. Describe a time when you coached someone successfully to do something challenging? What did you do. What did that feel like? What did you learn from this? In what areas would you like to do more coaching?

2. Tell me about a time when you have received can-do coaching. What did it help you to accomplish? What capacities did it help you discover in yourself?

3. Who is the best coach you currently have in your life? Tell me a story about this person as a coach. It may be a time when they coached you or you saw them coach someone else. What did they do that makes them a can-do coach? What do you most appreciate about this person?

Compelling Communication

Compelling communication is essential to the success of any endeavor or organization. Compelling communication occurs when information is shared in ways that enhance the relationships among people and their ability to do a good job. It occurs when conversation, dialogue or inquiry is open, honest, authentic and action oriented. It serves to strengthen relationships, to focus on the work to be done, and to convey a sense of caring and commitment.

Compelling communication is a two-way street. It involves sincere listening as well as open expression of ideas and opinions. When people feel in the know, have the information needed to do their job, and feel listened to and heard, they are better able to collaborate and co-create. Compelling communication gives people a sense of connection and belonging. It enables people to work together in ways that are mutually satisfying and inspiring. It is the backbone of organizational success.

1. Tell me about a time when compelling communication allowed you and another person to really connect and to work together exceptionally well. What was the situation? What was it about you, the other person, and the communication that made this possible?

2. Consider the various forms of communication within this organization.

   - Which are most effective in providing people with information to do their jobs?
   - Which most foster a sense of connection and belonging?

- Which most enable people to work together in ways that are mutually satisfying and inspiring?

3. Imagine that you've arrived at work tomorrow morning to find that a miracle happened. Compelling communication is now the only form of communication within our organization.

   - What is different?
   - How did we get here?
   - How does it feel?

Community Service

When organizations are at their best they support their local communities by offering their employees a wide array of alternatives for community service. Programs such as educational outreach, speakers' bureaus, adopt-a-school, and financial contributions all demonstrate an organization's commitment to the community in which it does business. The organization, the communities, and employees all benefit. Employees who volunteer for community service get inspired and energized by helping socially dedicated groups achieve their goals. Medical studies show that participation in community service increases peoples' sense of well-being. Their immune systems are actually strengthened by volunteer service! Community service is a tremendous opportunity for employee renewal while enhancing community capacity.

1. Describe a time when you did some meaningful community service. What was the high point of this experience? What did it feel like? What was your contribution?

2. What resources does your organization have that would benefit the community? How have your organization and the community cooperated meaningfully in the past?

3. Dream into the future . . . your organization and your community have a wonderful mutual partnership. What does this look like? What three things might have been done in order to create this partnership?

No Limits to Cooperation

We are living in a time in which there are no real limits to the possibilities for cooperation. The telecommunications capacity of organizations and indeed, the world, creates this limitless arena of potential cooperation. People around the globe can communicate and cooperate in ways that, just a short time ago, were barely even imagined. And the results can change our world.

Cooperation requires open communication and commitment to common purpose. It enables people with diverse interests to co-create and to find mutual satisfaction in shared processes and practices. It allows people and groups to maintain their separate and unique identities, while at the same time contributing to the achievement of a larger purpose.

1. When have you had a sense of wonder, surprise, or delight because cooperation in this organization had gone beyond anticipated limits? Tell a story about this time. Who was involved? What did you most value about them and about yourself in this situation?

2. Tell me about a time when you were a part of an exceptional cooperation with a customer or customer group. How did this happen? What made it so special? What did you learn from the experience?

3. When has new technology helped to facilitate and further cooperation in this organization? What was that experience like? What hope does it give you for the future?

4. Imagine that your organization has capitalized on cooperation in every form . . . that cooperation flourishes

among departments, teams, with customers, with suppliers, etc... and that this cooperation may take forms that are local, national, and global . . . What do you see happening in the organization? What's different and how do you know it?

Culture as Strategic Advantage

Every organization's culture is unique and special in some way. Every organization has its patterns and stories – "the way we do things around here" – that seem to stick with the organization forever, through thick and thin.

High-performing organizations are different than many organizations because they consciously create cultures, which support people in doing their jobs both effectively and enjoyably. They consciously develop those cultures in ways that are strategically different or better than their competition.

When approached with this kind of consciousness, an organization's culture becomes a strategic advantage. It helps attract and retain empowered and skilled employees who contribute to the excellence of their products and services.

1. When you think back to your beginnings with this organization, what were your most positive and powerful first impressions? What first attracted you to the organization and its people?

2. When you reflect on your time with this organization, what is the greatest contribution it has made to you and your life?

3. When you think of organizations that you consider to the best employers in your community or profession, what is it about their culture that makes them attractive to you? How might we create more of that quality within our own culture?

Customer Loyalty

Thriving organizations create and maintain exceptional levels of customer loyalty. Loyal customers are great customers. They assume good will. They provide information and time that helps us give them what they need. They share great ideas. They invite new customers.

Customer loyalty is something we earn. We earn it by listening to what our customers want, and if possible exceeding their expectations...by treating them with genuine respect and caring...by creatively anticipating ways in which products and services can become more and more customer-friendly.

It is cheaper and more satisfying to keep a customer than to find a new one. By earning customer loyalty, we build ourselves a competitive edge, which puts us in a leadership position and keeps us there in the future.

1. Think of a time when you were a customer, a very loyal customer: It could be of a large organization, or it could be of a neighborhood babysitter.

    - What were the most significant things that this person or organization did to earn your loyalty in the first place?
    - How did they learn about what was important to you? How did they stay current with your needs, as time went on?
    - Describe an episode when this loyalty was tested yet sustained. What did your provider do to keep you engaged, and if necessary rebuild the relationship?

2. Put yourself in the shoes of one of our most loyal customers.

   - How would they describe us to a prospective
     new customer?
   - Why would they say they're so committed to
     our products, our services, and us?

3. Suppose this organization could choose just three things to do
   more of, or do differently, in order to dramatically enhance
   our customers' loyalty. What would they be?

Participatory Decision-Making

When people know that their voice is being heard in a decision-making process, they feel respected, and they feel at the center of things. Everyone affected by a decision has different information to offer. Frequently, the best decisions are made inclusively, drawing upon a wide variety of information and ideas from a wide variety of people. Participatory decision-making builds trust and a sense of community. It leads to commitment; and it results in cooperative action.

1. Describe a time when you were involved in a participatory decision-making process in which everyone felt respected.

    - What was the high point of this process?
    - What made it successful?
    - How were you included or how did you contribute to the inclusiveness?
    - How did people know their voices were heard?

2. When you have been involved in an effective, inclusive decision-making process, what have you most valued about that process? What have you valued about the way people related to one another? How did participation improve the decisions made?

3. Where in the organization is participatory decision-making at its best? What contributes to it? How does it work?

4. What 2-3 things can we do to enhance participatory decision-making organization wide?

Strength in Diversity

When organizations are at their best, they capitalize on the strength of diversity. They hire and appreciate employees who bring different experiences, expertise, and ways of thinking to the organization. They build teamwork and cooperation on the strength of diversity – the ability to honor differences in the service of shared vision.

Diverse teams offer the strength and flexibility that comes from sharing multiple ways of looking at an issue, a strength which is available at any time. When we work in diverse groups, our learning about the world and each other is enriched by a cornucopia of perspectives. When we appreciate differences, we broaden trust and respect for individuals. The strength of diversity leads us to greater personal awareness, significantly better teamwork and greater organization agility.

1. Describe a time when you were part of a diverse team which really benefited from its diversity. How did you learn about each other's unique gifts and differences? What was special about what this group achieved?

2. Tell me about a time you had a wonderful working relationship with someone different from yourself. What was the high point of this relationship? What did you learn from this relationship?

3. Imagine into the future... your organization is one which honors and respects diversity... due to this, it benefits tremendously... it offers a special sensitivity to a diverse and large customer base... What do you see in this organization? What is it like walking around the halls of this organization?

Environmental Friendliness

We are part of an amazing web of life we call nature. Nature provides us with the air we breathe, the food we eat, the water we drink. Indeed, the resources used to create our products all come from the environment. The healthier the environment is, the healthier we all are. A clean environment in which plants and animals thrive benefits us all. Environmentally friendly action helps preserve public health. Action in favor of the environment can be very satisfying.

1. Tell about a time that you felt a profound connection to nature. What was that like? What do you take with from that experience?

2. When have you been a part of or seen this organization do something positive for the environment? Who was involved? What do you appreciate most about these people and this work?

3. If there were two things you would like to see this organization do that would benefit the environment, what would they be?

4. Imagine fifty years into the future: all of our pressing environmental issues have been solved. Perhaps cars are made of a soybean-based plastic and run on solar power. Nuclear waste can be broken down into harmless elements. Deforestation has been reversed, etc . . . What role might this organization have played in helping to build this healthy world?

Financial Responsibility

An organization and its members thrive when their financial decisions and actions are linked to – even driven by their core values. Organizations that endure over long periods of time are characterized by a sense of financial responsibility that is linked to social responsibility. They operate with the awareness that financial well-being means balancing the needs of customers, employees, shareholders, and the communities in which they operate.

Financial responsibility is good business and it is everyone's business.

Setting priorities, doing things right the first-time, and being aware of the costs of doing business is financial responsibility. As we are financially responsible for our work and its contribution to the organization as a whole, we contribute to our organization's well-being, and in turn to our own financial security and future with the organization.

1. Describe a time when you felt you exhibited a clear sense of financial responsibility. What was the situation and what did you do? What was the result of your financial responsibility?

2. Tell about a time in your life when you took steps to become more financially responsible. What did you do? What did this do for you? What was the high point of these changes?

3. Describe a time when you were involved in a group in this organization whose decisions and actions solidly demonstrated financial responsibility. How did this integrity help the group? What was high point of being involved in this group? What

were the decision-making processes like? What were the results?

Fun at Work

Organizations, at their best, are fun places to work. People enjoy each other and their work. They take their work and their customers seriously and themselves lightly. The work environment is charged with positive interaction and good humor. Sometimes, these interactions can be hilarious and endearing. A good laugh can break tension, make re-focusing easy, and offer new perspectives. High quality work can have a playful quality in which creativity and productivity flow. Levity and seriousness blend together in a beautiful dance.

1. Tell about a time that was particularly fun at work. What was the high point of this time? What made it fun?

2. Talk about a working relationship that is especially fun. How did this relationship develop? What do you most appreciate about this person?

3. Tell about a creative time at work. What did part did fun play? What did you accomplish?

One Big Hope

We live in a time of remarkable change, a time for re-thinking relationships among groups, organizations, and communities of all kinds. Daily, we see historic changes around the globe . . . the ending of apartheid in South Africa; the collapse of totalitarian regimes and the Cold War; the rapid spread of global communications; the birth of millions of grassroots organizations joining in the fight against global poverty and environmental decline. These and other global changes signal an open moment in world history – a time for great hope.

1. As you reflect on the shifts happening in the world, in your profession and in your life, tell me about one shift that for you generates hope – one that serves to nurture your hope in the possibility of building a better world.

2. In what ways are you and your colleagues responding – at work or in your community – to this one big hope?

3. Reflect on the world today through the eyes of your grandparents. What would they say are the most important values to carry into the future? What would they tell you to do about it?

Integrity in Action

When organizations are at their best there is no question of integrity. People are clear about their values and intentions, and they act consistently with them. Perhaps the most common explanation of integrity is to walk the talk or, in more contemporary terms, to be sure that the "audio and video match!" Integrity in action is essential for partnership, cooperation and doing meaningful work. It involves doing business with honesty. Integrity in action is a powerful expression of self-respect and care for colleagues and customers.

1. When have you felt that your actions have spoken for the best in who you are? What made this possible?

2. Who, in this organization, do you admire for walking their talk? Tell a story that illustrates this person's integrity in action.

3. Today, we spent a lot of time in meaningful and inspiring conversation. What three things could you do when you leave here that would be in alignment with the values and hopes we have talked about?

Joy in a Job Well-done

When people are fully engaged in their work and respect the people they work with, they enjoy what they are doing. It shows in the quality of their work. High performance is fun. The achievement of excellent results creates satisfaction and even joy. People want to be on a winning team, to work with others who respect them, and enjoy what they are doing. When this organization is at its best, employees are encouraged to unleash their imagination and energy, which makes work more rewarding, fulfilling, and joyful.

1. Recall a time when you did a good job and felt contentment and joy. What were you doing? What made it joyful? What did you appreciate about the people you were working with?

2. What one or two things might you or your colleagues do to invite more joy into the workplace?

Let's Do It

Being competitive in the world today can mean a hearty workload for those involved. The discipline to get things done creates momentum. In groups, sometimes we put aside our personal agendas to create a let's do it attitude. The focus on action can be magical, as we discover great capacity within ourselves to break through with resiliency and to achieve surprising results.

1. What has been a high point in your career, when you had honed your sense of self-discipline? What good things came out of that period of time? What were you doing to build and maintain that discipline?

2. When have you been involved in a group which kept its eyes on the prize – that maintained a let's do it attitude, and, because of this approach, achieved a lot? What was the high point of working in that group? What did you discover working in that group?

3. Who in this organization gets you into a let's do it mode? Tell a story about when they have done this. What makes working with them special?

Inspirational Leadership

People work best in the presence of inspirational leadership. When leaders exhibit enthusiasm and commitment to the task or project, people will "go the extra mile" and do whatever it takes to get the job done. Inspirational leaders bring out the best in people, they engage people in creating the organization's vision and values, in setting goals and objectives and in designing work processes. Inspirational leaders balance the needs and interests of employees, customer and the business. They encourage excellence in others as well as pursuing it themselves. They lead by example and demonstrate integrity in all that they do.

1. Recall a time when you worked with someone you considered to be an inspirational leader. Describe the situation. What made it inspirational for you? Who was the leader and what did she or he do that inspired you?

2. What do you most value and appreciate about leadership in your organization?

3. When people are in leadership positions, what two or three things can they do that will help you be the best you can be?

Irresistable Leadership

Organizations are at their best when they are leadership rich; when leadership is shared among people at all levels of the organization; and when leadership challenges people to go beyond what they believe is possible. Irresistible leadership engages peoples' hearts, minds and hands in the service of the organization's vision and core values. It creates a compelling call – a situation that invites people to join in, commit to and give their best. Irresistible leadership grows out of relationships that are trusting and challenging; supportive and provocative; visionary and practical.

1. Tell me about a time when you were inspired by irresistible leadership. What was the situation?

   - What made it irresistible?
   - Who was involved?
   - What did each person do to contribute to the strength of the situation?
   - What did you learn from this situation about leadership?

2. Tell me about a time when you where the source of irresistible leadership.

   - What created the sense of irresistible leadership?
   - How did you feel at this time?
   - How did others respond?

Continuous Learning

In a changing world, the competitive edge goes to organizations that can change, grow, or learn faster than others do. When at their best, organizations embrace continuous learning and become learning organizations in which people continuously challenge themselves to move out of their comfort zone, think in new ways, and acquire new knowledge and experiment with new ways of working.

Continuous learning creates an exciting work environment, full of creative possibilities for the organization and its members. It stimulates people to go beyond the usual to discover and create better, more financially and socially effective ways of doing things.

1. What most appeals to you about the concept of continuous learning?

2. Describe an organization or environment you've been in that has most inspired you and others to want to learn.

   - What made this such a favorable place for learning?
   - How did you and others grow and change, as a result of being in this environment?
   - What contributions were you able to bring back to one another, the organization, or the world at large, as a result of having been part of this system?

3. Every time we learn, we become bigger people. Even if we learn something that seems to have nothing to do with our

work, the changes we experience as we learn makes a difference in our work performance.

- What are your personal learning challenges – the things that you're curious about, that you'd like to learn more about, that will help you to become a bigger human being?
- In what ways will you change, as you grow into these new aspects of who you are?
- How do you see this new you contributing within our organization?

Organization Design

High-performing organization designs promote meaningful interactions within and across their entire system. They deliver high-quality products and services in a timely fashion. Their structures are flexible. They encourage individuals and departments to work across lines and positions – to adapt and respond to changing customer requirements, technologies, and regulations. They support people in identifying and seizing unexpected or unplanned strategic opportunities.

High-performing organizations' structures are also resilient. They serve the organization's purpose and principles. They create a "container" in which people can work together effectively, through good times and bad.

When they are at their best, organizational designs are economically, socially, and environmentally pragmatic. They nurture the life-giving qualities, and help people to live up to the organization's calling: its greatest contribution to the community, industry, and world.

1. Tell me about a time when this organization's structure most supported you in implementing our core purpose, vision, and values.

2. Describe an organization that you've seen, heard of, or experienced, whose structure was both flexible and resilient. What effect did this structure have on the organization's employees? Its customer relationships? Its products and services? Its financial performance? Its ability to achieve its vision?

3. What metaphor would you use to describe that organization's structure? (For example, you might say the organization was like a spider plant. It had an intentionally small central organization, with mini-organizations – or "chutes" – that would spring out every time a new product or service was launched.)

4. What can we learn from this organization you've just described? What might we borrow from its structure, in order to heighten the health and vitality of our organization?

Ownership

Organizations work best when everyone thinks, acts and feels that they are empowered owners of the company. A sense of ownership is highest when people share a vision for the business, and have freedom and authority to take action and to influence change. People who feel like owners take responsibility for the good of customers and the organization as a whole.

1. Describe a time when you felt and acted like an owner within your team, or of this organization.

   - What was it about you, the situation, and the organization that supported you in feeling this way?
   - What affect did that sense of ownership have on your feelings about your work? On your actions?

2. Describe an organization that you've seen, heard of, or experienced that does exceptionally well at promoting a sense of ownership among its employees, customers, and other stakeholders.

   - What do they do that's the same or different from the way we do our business?
   - What lessons do they have to teach us, that would help us create a greater sense of shared ownership throughout our organization?

Exceptional Partnership

Organizations are changing. Networks, virtual, and chaotic organizations are replacing traditional forms of organizing (such as hierarchy and centralized structures). These new forms of organizing call us to new ways of working together. Authoritarian leadership is giving way to participation. Patriarchy is giving way to partnership.

Organizations, at their best, encourage exceptional partnerships in which all parties have equal voice and share responsibility for co-creating the organization and its future. Partnerships require honesty, trust, respect and a focus on common interest; as well as a willingness to respect differences and agree to disagree. Exceptional partnerships result when all parties mutually gain from the relationship.

1. Tell me about the most exceptional partnership that you've ever been part of. What made it exceptional?

2. If you think of a partnership as a play, with each stage of the relationship being a different act, what are the major themes of each act?

3. Imagine all the possibilities for new and enhanced partnerships within this organization. What are the three most compelling opportunities for partnership that you see . . . those which promise the most unprecedented results for you and the organization and what must we do to realize the promise of these partnership responsibilities?

Union-Management Partnership

Exceptional organizations understand the value of true partnership between unions and management – a partnership in which differences are recognized and respected, and common ground is the focus of work together. A true union-management partnership benefits both the company and the unions as union and non-union employees work side-by-side to enhance organizational effectiveness, union strength, and the quality of work life for all employees.

When organizations are at their best, union-management partnership is a daily practice, an attitude, and a way of doing business.

People work best when their union and organization are in harmony, when guidance from the two organizations is in alignment, and when both the union and management support employee well-being.

1. Describe the time when you felt the greatest sense of alignment and partnership between unions and management within this organization. How did it come to pass? What impact did that partnership have on you, the unions, and the organization as a whole?

2. Tell me about a time when you participated in a process or an activity that reflected the union-management partnership. What was the situation? How was the partnership carried out? What was the result?

3. As union-management partnership develops within this organization, what impact will it have on this organization

five years from today?

- How are we organized?
- How do we develop and enhance our products and services?
- How do decisions get made?
- How do things feel?

Creating and Sustaining Positive Energy

Organizations work best when they are vibrant, alive and fun. You know, when the joint is jumping! You can sense that the spirit of the organization is vital and healthy and that people feel pride in their work. Everyone builds on each other's successes, a positive can-do attitude is infectious and the glow of success is shared. What's more, this positive energy is appreciated and celebrated so it deepens and lasts.

1. Tell me about a time when you experienced positive energy that was infectious. What was the situation? What created the positive energy? How did it feel to be a part of it? What did you learn?

2. If positive energy were the flame of the organization, how would you spark it? How would you fuel it to keep it burning bright?

Praise is the Fuel of High Performance

In vital and alive organizations praise and appreciation are the norm. Praise is recognized as the fuel of high performance and is given freely. Colleagues, customers and managers all share in the process of giving and receiving praise. Spontaneous praise contributes to self-confidence and sets the tone for positive working relationships.

Satisfaction, enthusiasm and commitment rise in an environment of praise and appreciation. More work gets done and more people have fun when praise is practiced throughout the organization.

1. When has there been a flow of sincere praise and appreciation such that people have wanted to stay in this organization? What generated this praise? How did it come about? What effect did it have on the people you were involved with?

2. Who can you currently think of whom would benefit from a bit of sincere praise? What do you appreciate about what that person does?

3. Describe a relationship in which praise flows freely. Who is involved? What makes it okay to give praise? How does frequent praise impact the relationship?

Quality Moments

It has been said that quality is job one. Everyone recognizes and appreciates quality when they experience it. People feel a sense of pride when they have contributed to a quality moment – a time when their efforts made a difference, a time when a product or service delighted the customer, a time when it was easy to do the right thing.

Quality moments in customer service, technical assistance, sales, or manufacturing all lead to employee pride and customer satisfaction – a winning combination. Our success – both now and in the future – depends upon our ability to continually and consistently create quality moments in the eyes of our customers.

1. Tell me about a time when you were on the receiving end of a quality moment – when a product or service delighted you, as a customer.

    - What was it like?
    - How did it feel?
    - How did that experience enhance or change your relationship with the person or organization who provided it?

2. Describe a quality moment that you participated in creating – either in this organization, or in the past.

    - What was it about you, your team, and the product or service you delivered that allowed this moment to take place?
    - How did you know it was a quality moment?
    - What was the customer's response to the experience?

3. What can we learn from these experiences of quality moments? How can we take what you know and apply it to our organization, to create more of that winning combination of employee pride and customer satisfaction?

Recognition

It is meaningful to be recognized and appreciated for work done well. Recognition gives us a sense of satisfaction and community. When others care about and value our contribution, it inspires us to strive for excellence. Giving recognition can often be as rewarding as receiving it. When we see excellence in another and recognize it, we see possibilities for our own excellence.

When organizations are centers of recognition and celebration, people feel challenged to give their best, to learn and to contribute to the well-being of others. Recognition creates a work environment where cooperation, partnership and teamwork thrive.

1. Tell about a time when you received recognition, appreciation, or acknowledgment for your work. Describe the situation. What did you do? How were you recognized? How did it make you feel?

2. Tell about a time when you appreciated and honored someone else's contribution. What was that like? What did you do?

3. Describe types of recognition that would inspire you to strive for excellence. Why would these types of recognition be meaningful to you?

4. It's sometime in the future and your grandchildren are being told a story about you at work. What are you most proud of that you would like them to hear about?

Respect for People

Organizations that are recognized as great places to work are characterized by an uncompromising respect for people. When respect for people is demonstrated in personal interactions and in management practices throughout the organization, it creates a positive work environment in which people feel safe to express themselves and to take risks toward innovation and learning.

People feel respected when they are involved in dialogue and decision-making, when they are listened to, when they are valued for their ideas and opinions, and when they have opportunities to fully participate in achieving the organization's goals. Respect for people is contagious. People who feel respected in turn respect others – colleagues and customers. Respect for people nurtures self-confidence, enhances teamwork and facilitates organization success.

1. Tell me about a time when you experienced a strong sense of respect from another person – colleague, customer or friend. What gave you that feeling of respect?

2. Think of an organization you've heard of or experienced that demonstrates uncompromising respect for people. Tell me a story that illustrates that respect. What effect did that story have on you?

3. Suppose we were to incorporate the best from the story you just described into our organization. What would we do the same, do more of, or do differently, if we were to live from their wisdom?

Role Clarity

When organizations are at their best, people clearly understand and are committed to their unique role in achieving the organization's purpose. Understanding how their work fits with the work of others in the organization gives people a sense of connection and of significance. It helps people bring their best to the work at hand.

Role clarity results from dialogue and discussion: taking the time to talk about who does what and how the processes, procedures and relationships interrelate to meet the needs of customers.

1. Describe a time when a sense of role clarity helped you perform at exceptional levels within an organization. In what way did having a clear role help you perform at your best?

2. Reflecting on this time when you had a sense of role clarity, how was it created? Who was involved and what did they do? What did you do that contributed to the sense of role clarity?

3. Imagine you arrived at work tomorrow morning and everybody's role clarity was as good or better as in the group that you just described.

   - What's the same or different from a week ago?
   - What's changed in people's performance?
   - How have the organization's products and services been transformed?

Root Cause of Success

Successful people, teams and organizations spend time studying success. They know how other people and organizations achieve extraordinary results and they know their own strengths and limitations. They work from strengths in ways that make their limitations irrelevant. Finding the root cause of success serves to ignite a sense of the possible. Focusing on the root cause of success fosters creativity, builds relationships and informs future actions with positive possibilities. It provides a rich collection of ideas and practices to be enhanced and spread throughout the organization.

1. What is your sense of the root cause of the ongoing success of this organization? Tell a story that illustrates something about how this root cause takes effect.

2. When, in your work, have you felt most connected to this root cause? What effect did this sense of connection have on the work you were doing?

3. What work do you see to be done that will reaffirm this root cause of success? What three steps could be taken to initiate this process?

Seamless Service

Seamless service is service that creates exceptional results, delights our customers, and brings joy to our work. Individual activities and processes are invisible to the untrained eye. They involve meticulous understanding of and attention to customer desires . . . smooth and accurate pass-offs from person to person and function to function . . . a shared focus on doing the right thing right . . . a common commitment to be easy to do business with, and to show they care.

1. Describe a time when you experienced seamless service as a customer. What was the situation? How did that experience shape your relationship with the organization and its products or services?

2. Think of a time when you have been involved in providing seamless service – either here or in another organization.

   - What was it about you, your co-workers, and the organization that facilitated that seamless service?
   - What impact did that service have on customer relations? On the people who delivered the service? On the organization's overall financial performance?
   - What key aspects of that service can we incorporate into our organization on an ongoing basis?

Strategic Advantage

When organizations are at their best, people know and build upon the organization's key strategic advantages: qualities, products and services that make them both different and better than their competition. Almost anything can become a strategic advantage: the organization's culture . . . a committed workforce . . . unique products or services . . . financial strength . . . a capacity to be "first to market" with breakthroughs and innovations . . . being exceptionally easy to do business with.

Strategic advantages help organizations to win . . . to be the best they can possibly be. When they are conscious and well communicated, strategic advantages can also be sources of pride for an organization's employees, customers, and communities. They can help people to feel a sense of ownership and purpose – a sense of their unique place in the world in which they work.

1. What do you believe are this organization's most significant strategic advantages?

2. Which of these strategic advantages gives you the greatest sense of pride and purpose? Why?

3. Consider the collective impact of all of our strategic advantages on such things as our financial performance, position in the community, position in the industry, and future potential. What has been the most significant positive outcome of our use of these advantages?

4. How would you envision us building upon or leveraging them so that they would become even greater advantages in the future?

Strategic Opportunities

Organizations today exist in an ever-changing sea of possibilities. Changes in an organization's business environment – regulations, customer requirements, technology, and competition – create opportunities for strategic change within the organization. The ability to act on strategic opportunities – possibilities that build upon the organization's strengths and that create an advantage in the marketplace – is essential to an organization's success. Strategic opportunities help organizations create markets for their products or services – often before customers or competitors have even dreamed of the possibilities.

1. What trends and changes are you seeing in the world that excite you and give you a sense of confidence in the possibilities for the organization's future?

2. Given these trends, imagine our organization ten years from today. What do you see? Be creative as you answer questions such as:

    - What industries do we serve? Who are our key customers?
    - What products or services do we offer?
    - How many employees do we have? With what skills? At how many locations?
    - How do we do our work?

3. Now, looking back from the position of ten years hence, describe the history of how the organization got to where it is. What decisions were made ten years ago in order to get us to where we are?

Winning Teamwork

In today's complex and ever-changing business environment, teamwork is an essential ingredient for success. In high performance organizations teamwork fosters collaboration across departments and functions, and results in the organization's being easy to do business with.

Winning teamwork requires common goals, open communication, and full participation in planning and decision-making. Most people work best in a team environment where enthusiasm and team spirit are high, where ideas and information are shared, and where team members work together to accomplish common goals. It has been said that the results of teamwork are greater than the sum of the parts. The synergy that comes from winning teamwork adds value to team members, customers and the organization.

1. What are the qualities in your existing team that most foster enthusiasm, information sharing, and collaboration towards common goals?

2. Describe the best, most winning teamwork that you have ever seen or been a part of.

    • What was it about that team's activities that caused you to define them as the best?
    • What were all the conditions that allowed that winning teamwork to emerge?

3. What can we do to foster winning teamwork at an even higher and more consistent level, throughout our organization?

Technology that Serves

When organizations are at their best, they create and employ technology in service of their higher purpose – their vision, values and day-to-day operating goals. This technology that serves takes on a life-giving quality for the organization, its employees, and its customers. It liberates people and processes. It greatly enhances performance, creativity, and quality.

1. Describe the single most significant contribution that technology currently makes to you, our organization, and our customers. In what ways are your work and your quality of life enhanced through access to this technology?

2. What are the three most important enhancements you would wish for in our current technology, in order to have it be more of service to you and our customers?

3. Imagine an organization in which technology only exists in service of the people who are within and outside the organization.

   - What types of technology are employed?
   - What kind of training and development precedes people's use of the technology?
   - How is the technology maintained, updated, and enhanced over time?

Visions of a Better World

World-class organizations exist to serve a vision of a better world. Their purpose, principles and people are aligned with the vision. Products and services are created to realize the vision. People within such organizations are energized and inspired by possibilities for a better world.

When work is in service to a larger purpose it is life-giving and compelling. People want to contribute. They get great satisfaction from knowing that their work and their organization are positive forces in the world.

1. When have you most felt like your work was part of a positive force in the world, when you felt an alignment among your principles, purpose, and practices? Tell a story about what you were doing.

2. What do you see today (not future possibilities, but beginning to happen right now) that gives you hope for the future? This could be something on a global scale, or a personal experience. It could have to do with social or political events, or it could have to do with what you've experienced in this organization or your community.

3. If a genie appeared right now in front of you, and offered to grant you three wishes (without worrying how they would be fulfilled) to heighten vitality and effectiveness in this organization, what would these three wishes be? What do you wish for the organization and the people involved?

Shared Vision

Organizations succeed when people throughout the organization share and work from a common vision. Shared vision guides actions and decisions and provides a sense of how to proceed in times of change. Shared vision excites people and inspires them to contribute their best and to collaborate for the success of the whole organization. When people are aligned around a shared vision, they are clear about where the company is going, how it will contribute to its customers and what it will take to succeed. They understand how their work serves the big picture – the organization's success; and they feel they are at the center of things, making a significant contribution.

1. Describe a time when you felt most involved in the big picture of the organization. Tell me about the situation. How did you know you were involved in the big picture? What about the situation brought out the best in you?

2. Reflecting back on the situation you just described, what did you learn about how to create shared vision within a team, department or whole organization?

Work/Family Balance

In today's world most of us are juggling and balancing many different responsibilities – at work and in our families. When we are at our best we can easily balance work and family. When we value work/family balance we organize both work and family life to eliminate wasted time, to focus on key priorities and to cooperate to achieve shared goals. When organizations are at their best they encourage work/family balance in a variety of ways: day care centers, optional time off, job sharing, etc. It takes personal commitment and organizational support to sustain work/family balance.

1. Tell me about a time, recently, in which you experienced a comfortable sense of work/family balance. What contributed to it? What did you do to create the sense of balance?

2. What is it about your organization that best supports you in creating work/family balance?

3. Thinking about the organization, what one thing could be done that would help you create a better work/family balance?

Men and Women Working Together

Most of us regularly work with people from both genders. In this context, positive, constructive across-gender working relationships are essential. Successful organizations are characterized by partnerships between men and women: across-gender relationships in which men and women contribute from their strengths, and are recognized and feel valued for their contribution. Men and women working together produce results which invite others into greater openness and creativity; and demonstrate the potential for new ways of working and doing business.

1. Tell about a time you have been involved in a positive, effective, and life-affirming working relationship with someone of the other gender. How did this relationship get started?

    - Think back over the course of the relationship. What stands out as significant and meaningful high points?
    - How did you gain each other's respect and trust?

2. What do you value most about yourself that contributes positively to the relationships between men and women in the workplace?

3. What would you want to see more of so that your organization could support or improve across-gender working relationships?

4. What would you like the 21st century organization to look like with respect to across-gender relationships?

Encyclopedia of Positive Questions

SECTION 3

Ten Ways to Spread Appreciative Stories

A Romanian fable says, "stories have wings and they fly from mountain top to mountain top." Within organizations, this is indeed the case. Stories – be they good news stories, best practice stories, or crisis stories – spread throughout an organization. As they spread they teach about the way things are done within the organization; they inform action. Stories create the context we live and work within; they tell us how to behave within that context. For example, take the story about a Federal Express employee who rented a helicopter to deliver a package on-time. This story tells us much about the values and ways of working at Federal Express. It tells us that customers matter and on time delivery matters. It tells us that employees do whatever it takes to satisfy the customer. What do the stories in your organization tell you about your organization's values and ways of doing business?

Appreciative Inquiry focuses on what the organization does at its best and what gives life and a sense of vitality to its members. The more Appreciative Inquiry stories collected during the interview process can be spread, the more organization members can learn from the best of one another and the organization. Spreading Appreciative Inquiry stories enhances organizational learning, recognizes work well-done, and sets a tone of being the best. The following is a list of ways to spread AI stories.

1. Reports and Presentations – AI data and stories may be compiled into a report, which is circulated around the organization. Managers and employees have access to it and often use it as a source of creative alternatives. A written report can also serve as a catalyst for a large group meeting, known as an AI Summit. When used as advance reading for a Summit, a report can set an affirmative and hopeful tone for the meeting.

In lieu of a report, interviewers may make presentations about their findings to groups within the organization or as part of an Appreciative Inquiry Summit meeting. For example, if a group interviewed customers, a group interviewed community leaders and a group interviewed suppliers, each group might present their most surprising and inspiring findings to the large group.

The focus of either a report or presentation is to create a profile of the organization's positive core: those positive qualities, relationships, capabilities, etc. which make the organization uniquely itself.

2. Company History - Appreciative Inquiry data and stories make great input for a book on the company history. Organizations marking significant anniversaries, such as 50 years doing business or 10 years since the invention of a unique product, can derive great benefit from creating a book on the company history. Appreciative Interviews can be used to generate a rich collection of personal experiences and remembrances. The focus of such a document is to position history as a source of positive possibility and to compile the best of the past as a foundation for the future.

3. Company Newsletter - Appreciative Inquiry can be a rich source of stories for a company's regular newsletter. Organizations have often created special columns for the publication of the best of Appreciative Inquiry stories. Other organizations have created special editions and even new employee bulletins to spread information and stories generated via the interview process. In these ways an organization's best practices are made available to everyone.

4. Interviewer Focus Groups - A common practice is to bring interviewers together in groups of 8-12 to share highlights of their interviews. Interviewer focus groups create both an information-sharing and a narrative or story rich culture. They provide an opportunity for people to learn about what works well in different parts of the organization. They can be used to foster cross-functional learning and collaboration, to build relationships among newly merged organizations and to create a profile of the organization's positive core.

5. Storytelling Teams - Storytelling teams are groups of employees who are available to attend company meetings as well as outside events in order to share stories about the organization, its people and their achievements. They use Appreciative Interview data as the basis of their presentations. Often an organization embarking on an AI process will invite members of another organization which has used AI to share their experiences with the processes.

6. Video Highlights - Capturing the best of the interviews on video makes the AI experience accessible to many more people than just the interviewers. Highlight tapes may involve interviewers telling about the interviews they conducted and what they learned. Interviewees may also be videotaped telling what made the interview a significant experience for them, and sharing their success stories.

Highlight videos may be played in company cafeterias, at staff meetings and as part of employee training sessions. As the stories are told and retold on video they come alive again and are spread throughout the organization.

7. Story Wall or Poster Sessions - Imagine a wall in the company cafeteria, or in the lobby that is covered with posters of the stories collected during Appreciative Interviews. Each interviewer may make a poster or draw an illustration on the story wall that best illustrates their greatest learning or excitement from the interview process. Interview focus groups may be asked to collectively create a poster highlighting the most exciting and enlivening aspects of their interviews. The story wall is available for all to see. Anyone can interact with it by adding to the wall. The interview guide is readily available and anyone can do an interview and then add their discoveries to the wall. It can keep both the interviewing process and the storytelling process alive.

8. Intranet Site - As can be imagined, if we can spread stories on a wall, we can spread stories on the intranet. Organizations with intranets can create an AI web site for learning about AI and the many inspirational stories generated. Stories may be replaced frequently to keep the learning discussions fresh and to continually recognize the work of more and more people.

9. Meeting Starters - Many leaders, seeing the benefits of spreading positive stories, choose to start all meetings with good newstorytelling. One CEO asks team members to share magic moments at work since their last meeting. Another executive's office serves as the clearinghouse for positive stories. He selects one or two and reads them as openers for staff meetings. Opening meetings with AI stories creates an atmosphere of success and possibility. It sets a tone for creativity and cooperation. And it suggests that colleagues share in one another's successes.

10. Art Exhibition - Many members of organizations are artists. Most organizations are filled with poets, painters, singers, and musicians, writers, dancers, photographers and comedians. Given an opportunity they would gladly bring their talents to the expression of the organization's positive core. Having company artists listen in on interviewer focus groups and then creatively render the best of the organization in song, dance, paint and poetry sparks a sense of vitality and enthusiasm throughout the company. The exhibition can be as simple as space in the company cafeteria, or as special as a family reception to learn about the company.

Encyclopedia of Positive Questions

SECTION 4

How to Choose Affirmative Topics

Affirmative topic selection is the first step in an Appreciative Inquiry process. We believe the seeds of change are implicit in the very first questions we ask. Careful, thoughtful, and informed choice of topics is important, because it defines the scope of the inquiry and provides the framework for everything that follows. As we have said earlier, Appreciative Inquiry is founded in part on the principle that organizations move in the direction of what they study. If we study problems, we create problems. If we study possibilities, we create more possibilities. For this reason, topic choice is fateful.

Characteristics of Good Topics

You should select between three and five compelling, "juicy" topics, all of which meet the following criteria:

- They are *affirmative*, or stated in the positive.
- They are *desirable*. You would want to create more of it in your life at work or at home.
- You are *genuinely* curious about them, and would want to learn about them.
- They will take you *where you want to go*.

And as you proceed, remember the following principles:

- Human systems – people and organizations move in the direction of the images we hold of the future.

- Images *of the future are* informed by the conversations we have and the stories we tell.
- Conversations and sto*ries are* informed by the questions we ask, so . . .
- . . . the questions we ask are fateful.

SECTION 5

The Anatomy of A Positive Question

What is a positive (appreciative) question? How do we know it when we see it? What's the connection between what we create in our questions, and what we believe as practitioners of Appreciative Inquiry?

A positive question is an affirmatively stated question—a question that seeks to uncover and bring out the best in a person, a situation or an organization. It is constructed around a topic that has been selected by a person or group – a topic that is *fundamentally affirmative*. This should be a topic which they are trying to grow or develop in people or their organization.

Positive Appreciative Inquiry questions are generally structured as follows:

- The title of the affirmative topic;
- A lead-in, which introduces the topic and describes it as already existing;
- A series of sub-questions (usually two to four), which explore different aspects of the topic.

These are the structural qualities of a positive question. However, positive questions are usually *more than structure*. Following is a summary of the essential qualities that Appreciative Inquiry practitioners look for as they write their positive questions and construct their interview guides.

Lead-ins

Lead-ins are interviewees' first introduction to the affirmative topic of the inquiry. As such, they play a critical role in setting the tone for both questions and responses.

The more relaxed interviewees are, the greater the possibility for depth in their responses. So good lead-ins put people at ease with the topic at hand. They help them to consider the topic from different angles. In some cases, they define the topic, so that people can begin to consider when they have seen it.

Remember the old adage about the "half-full" and "half-empty" glass? When writing Appreciative Interview questions, we always assume that the glass is half-full: that the topic or quality that we're exploring already exists in the person, the organization, and the world. We see ourselves as detectives, trying to uncover and understand where the topic exists, why it exists, and how it can exist to a greater extent.

Quality lead-ins plant that half-full assumption in the mind of an interviewee. They talk about the topic or quality at its best. They describe the relationship between topics and the personal or organizational vitality that they're intended to enhance.

When an engine is out of gas, we sometimes need to "prime the pump" to help it use the fuel that's available. Most of us have been well-conditioned to think through what's wrong... to identify and solve problems. Thinking about our most positive and affirmative experiences and insights can be foreign – sometimes challenging. So we offer lead-ins to positive questions, in part, to help to prime the pump. Really good lead-ins can help interviewees to draw from the "fuel" of personal experience and insight, and to convert that into a boundless source of creativity, energy, and enthusiasm for the affirmative topic of inquiry.

At their best, lead-ins are truly compelling. They show interviewees the benefit of the quality that's being explored. Sometimes they paint pictures of the positive outcomes that are possible, when the quality is significantly present in an organization. They make people want more of that quality, within their organizations and within themselves.

High-quality lead-ins appeal to people, not just business. They speak to and resonate with the yearning for meaning that is so much a part of the human experience. They are personal and affective. A number of hard business topics – such as finance, strategy, and quality – are included in the list of sample questions. The lead-ins allow us to explore each of those topics from a human perspective. They help us to build bridges between the business' needs and our emotional needs for such things as a sense of pride, ownership, belonging, connection, and personal growth.

Most of us will do things just "because they are there." We may even do them well, just because "it's our job." But our greatest potential for positive performance exists when we have an emotional and spiritual stake in the task at hand.

In our quest to understand the qualities that "give life" to organizing and organizations, we must consider things from many angles. Simple attention to the more traditional measures of "success" within the world of business is not enough, if our goal is to mobilize people's hearts, souls, and spirits in the service of their work. Likewise, exclusive attention to people's affective natures will not help people to think more pragmatically and strategically about their work and their organization.

Great lead-ins set the stage for a "whole-brained" response to the questions that follow. They highlight the connection between "good thinking" and "good feeling" – a connection which must be internalized by the interviewee, if he or she is to offer the fullest, most creative, most meaningful response possible.

Sub-Questions

Individual sub-questions, which follow lead-ins in a "positive question," generally fall into one of three time frames: past; present; and future. Often, we include all three time frames, when we write a question; sometimes we focus on only one or two. By inquiring into different time frames, we help interviewees to place the topic in both their experience and their imagination.

Most good sub-questions invite people to participate actively in the process of both inquiry and creation. For example, we ask interviewees about times when they have experienced or seen the topic. We have them place themselves in the future, and then look back to consider how they got there. Some of the best sub-questions are those in which we ask interviewees to describe in detail the way that things looked, smelled, tasted, or felt. By asking for such tactile – even visceral – descriptions, we encourage them to enter the experience.

Both personal and tactile descriptions engage a part of interviewees' brains which is generally left behind during logical analysis. This more creative intelligence – which is seated in the right hemisphere of the brain – is unable to distinguish between imagination and reality. It is often more capable of generating a whole new series of positive possibilities than the part of the brain that is rooted in concrete past experience.

In a good appreciative interview, we're not just interested in the data – we're interested in the experience and the relationships. Perhaps the most discernible characteristic of a good positive question is that it invites people to tell stories and participate at that very human level.

Last but not least, good positive questions invite people to learn and make meaning from both their past experience and their ideal projections into the future. We invite them to dive deep into their memories... in some ways, to dissect them. Often these meaning making questions ask them to consider qualities about themselves, as well as the situation, which allowed an experience of "best" to emerge.

At their best, positive questions encourage people to consider and hear many different voices (for example, their own, their customers or suppliers, their community, etc.). From time-to-time, they actually ask people to "step into someone else's shoes" before they respond. This invitation to change their way of thinking seems to stretch the interviewees' imaginations, while also teaching compassion and respect for both differences and different ways of thinking and feeling.

Encyclopedia of Positive Questions

SECTION 6

Creating An Interview Guide

Once we have decided upon topics, lead-ins and questions, the next task is to create an interview guide, or protocol. A typical interview guide has three parts: stage-setting questions, topic questions, and conclusion questions. However, Appreciative Inquiry is a discipline that continues to grow as we discover new ways of doing things that work. This is not the only way to organize a successful interview guide – it is just one proven model.

Part 1: Stage-Setting Questions

These questions and the beginning of the interview are designed to initiate meaningful and inspiring conversation, to draw the participants into the process, and to open the doors of the appreciative parts of the psyche. Part 1 includes questions designed to allow interviewee and interviewer to build trust. As is common in Appreciative Inquiry, stage-setting questions invite storytelling. The questions ask the interviewee to draw on direct personal experience. Questions that work particularly well as stage-setting questions include:

- Please tell me about your initial attraction to the organization. What inspired you to join?
- Describe a high point experience – a time when you felt most alive and engaged in the organization.
- What do you value most about: yourself, your work, and your organization?

- What is the core factor that gives life to this organization – without it the organization would not be the same?

Part 2: Topic Questions

The second part of an interview provides an opportunity to inquire into those topics about which we are truly curious and want to grow in the organization. Thus, the second part of an interview guide involves topic questions. There is an endless universe of affirmative topics and positive questions. This section of the interview guide contains 3-5 topic questions.

The 3-5 topics cluster around a focal theme or purpose for the inquiry. For example, if the purpose of the inquiry is strategic planning, topics such as strategic advantage, best-in-class, and strategic opportunities might be selected. If the purpose of the inquiry is organization culture change, topics such as compelling communication, joy in a job well-done, teamwork and recognition might be selected. For a study of leadership we might use the topics of inspirational leadership, participatory decision-making and integrity in action.

Part 3: Conclusion Questions

The third part of an interview guide is the conclusion. Conclusion questions provide an opportunity to summarize and to place the learnings from the organization's positive history into a future vision. Questions that are appropriate for this part of the interview include:

- Looking toward the future, what are we called to become?
- What three wishes do you have for enhancing the health and vitality of the organization?
- If your wishes were realized and things were wonderful, what would be happening in this organization today?
- What are three positive macro trends happening in the world today and what new possibilities are they creating for this organization?
- Imagine that it is the year 2008 and we have just awakened after 6 years of sleep. And to our surprise, the organization is exactly as we always wished it were. What is different? What is happening that lets us know it is different?

As you can see, good conclusion questions are creative and invite imaginative responses. They seek real possibilities for the future.

Creating an interview guide can be an exciting task. What we ask determines what we "find." What we find determines how we talk. How we talk determines how we imagine together. How we imagine together determines what we achieve.

As you construct your interview guide, consider the following:

- Are your questions appropriate – yet a stretch for your organization?
- Are you genuinely curious to hear the answers?
- Do they "sing" to the people who will be interviewed?
- Will they take you where you want to go?

Finally, be courageous as you experiment with the sample questions included in this book. Make them yours. Have a good time.

SECTION 7

Sample Interview Guide

The following is a sample of a complete interview guide originally used to guide pre-work interviews for a Corporate Human Resources department's planning retreat.

XYZ CORPORATION INTERVIEW GUIDE

Your Name: _____

Interviewee's Name: _____

Date: _____

Introduction

Thanks for joining me here today, and for agreeing to be interviewed. Before we get started, let me take a minute to share with you what we're doing here in this interview, and why.

As you probably know, I am a member of XYZ's Corporate Human Resources Department. Later this month, our group will be meeting for a couple of days to take a look at who we are at our best – and to find ways we might organize in the future that will leverage our strengths to make us even better.

Between now and the retreat, all of us will be involved in what we call "Discovery." During this Discovery period, we are conducting interviews with other XYZ employees, customers, suppliers, and community members. We are also interviewing people from other organizations that have great reputations in the area of human resources management. We're trying to learn about what's best about XYZ Human Resources, as well as other human resource organizations. We want to know what's best, because we want to find ways to organize around the things that really work here and elsewhere. We want to be able to grow those things bigger and better. We want to use what we know works to become the best we can possibly be.

The questions I'm about to ask you are called appreciative questions. I am going to ask you about times when you have seen things working at their best, both in this organization and in other organizations you've known. Many times we try to ask about things that aren't working well – the problems – so that we can fix them. In this case, we try to find out about the things that are working – the successes – so that we can find out what works and do more of it.

So the best thing you can-do for me in this conversation is to think about, remember, and tell me details about the things you've seen, heard of, or imagined – either here or in other organizations – that really work.

Do you have any questions? *(Respond, then begin.)*

Opening

1. Tell me about a peak experience or high point in your professional life – a time when you felt most alive, most engaged, or really proud of yourself or your work. What was it about you, the situation, the organization, and/or the leadership that allowed that peak experience to emerge?

2. Tell me about your beginnings with XYZ.

   - What most attracted you to work here in the first place?
   - Once you were hired, what were your initial impressions?
   - Describe one of your earliest positive experiences with the organization, and how that reinforced your initial sense that this was a great place to work.

3. Think of a time when XYZ's Corporate Human Resources was at its absolute best . . . when our stakeholders (employees, customers, suppliers, and community members) easily saw who we really are and what we're really about. Tell me about it.

   - Who was involved and how did they contribute to the success?
   - What did you learn from that experience?

One Success at a Time

Many great successes are achieved by approaching something big with baby steps – for when they're thoughtfully planned and well-executed, little successes add up over time to significant results or impact. We in Human Resources promote sustained positive change within this flexible, dynamic organization by creating one success at a time in all that we do.

One success at a time means providing "win-win" solutions to even the smallest challenges. It means looking for, finding, promoting, and building upon what's working, so that the organization can learn to help itself. It means looking for satisfaction in a job well-done, and doing our work – whatever it may be – enthusiastically, competently, and with complete integrity.

1. Tell me about the one success you've had here at XYZ that brings you the greatest pride in having made a difference for a person, a department, or the organization as a whole.

    - What was it about the situation that most supported you in delivering this one success?
    - What was the immediate outcome?
    - What are the most positive long-term consequences of this one success – either tangible or intangible?
    - What does this experience teach you about yourself and XYZ as a whole? What conditions do we need to create, so that we can all deliver successes like this in the future?

2. It's three years from today. XYZ is featured in Fast Company

magazine as "one company to watch" for its consistent, steady, competent-yet-creative approach to human resources management. Why?

- What "big ticket" accomplishments have attracted the attention of this prestigious publication?
- What is it in the day-to-day operation of the Corporate Human Resources Department that makes it such an effective player in the larger organization?

Inviting the Extraordinary

In today's rapidly changing business environment, our organization's success depends on our collective capacity to invite the extraordinary.

When we are at our best, we in Corporate HR invite the extraordinary by creating vehicles for people to be at their best, and by blending old methods into new and different solutions. We invite the extraordinary by exploring and taking risks . . . by helping people look at things in new and different ways. We invite the extraordinary by serving as a conduit for new ideas, and boldly *inventing* new ways of working that establish industry-changing standards for excellence.

1. Describe the most extraordinary contribution that the Corporate Human Resources Department has made to this organization and its success.

    - How did it come about? (Consider background training/education, support and/or collaboration with peers, resources, outside support, etc.)
    - What were the circumstances that elevated that contribution from ordinary to extraordinary?
    - What does this episode teach us about inviting the extraordinary on an ongoing and continuous basis?

2. What's the most extraordinary thing that you'd personally like to accomplish, within the next two years? (It could be in your current job, or in a new job in this Department or

elsewhere in the organization.) What could the Corporate Human Resources Department do to support you in achieving that?

Closing

1. Imagine you had a magic wand, and you could have any three wishes granted, to build on the best of what the Corporate Human Resources Department already is, and to make the Department even stronger in the eyes of the larger organization. What would those wishes be? *(Please – THINK BIG!)*

   -
   -
   -

2. What's been the most important thing you've learned – or perhaps re-learned – about Corporate HR and yourself, as a result of this conversation we've just shared?

Thanks so much for taking the time to share your thoughts and feelings with me. I've learned a lot about you, this organization, and XYZ's future possibilities, as a result of this conversation.

In order for our Department to make full use of all your thoughts and ideas, we'll need to talk over some of the details of what you've shared when we gather later this month. I'm guessing this won't be a big deal for you, since the things you've shared are examples of XYZ and other organizations at their best.

Still, I want to be sure that I'm representing you in a way that you're comfortable with. So I'd like to ask you to take a few minutes to read over my notes. Let me know if I've misunderstood anything you've said, or written it in a way that feels uncomfortable for you. Also, let me know if there's anything in those notes that you're unwilling to have quoted or attributed to you, in a public setting.

(either read or let them read notes . . .)

So again, thanks for your time. This conversation has been really interesting for me – and it will help me work with my group to make XYZ's Corporate Human Resources Department the best it can possibly be.

Encyclopedia of Positive Questions

SECTION 8

Build Your Own Interview Guides

The blank interview guides on the following pages are templates to help you create your own interview guides.

There are spaces to insert the name of your organization or team, the specifics of who you are interviewing and the timeline, along with the interview questions you have chosen from the Encyclopedia of Positive Questions. Simply fill in the blanks and you will have a great interview guide.

Or, if you prefer, use these templates to create your own completely home-grown interview guides.

Encyclopedia of Positive Questions

INTERVIEW GUIDE

Your Name: _____

Interviewee's Name: _____

Date: _____

Introduction

Thanks for joining me today, and for agreeing to be interviewed as part of the _____ *(name of organization or team)* inquiry. Before we get started, let me take a minute to share with you what we're doing in this interview, and why we're doing it.

Insert textual description of what the inquiry is about, why, for whom, timelines, etc.

_____

_____

_____

_____

_____

_____

Between _____ and _____, we are conducting interviews with _____ *(list the people being interviewed; e.g., employees, customers, suppliers, and community members).* We are interviewing people from other organizations that have a great reputation. We want to learn about what they do best and how they do it. We want to know

what works best, because we want to find ways to organize around the things that really work, both here and elsewhere.

The questions I'm about to ask you are called appreciative questions. I am going to ask you about times when you have seen things working at their best, both in this organization and in other organizations you've known. Many times we try to ask about things that aren't working well – the problems – so that we can fix them. In this case, we try to find out about the things that are working – the successes – so that we do more of it.

So the best thing you can-do for me in this conversation is to think about, remember, and tell me details about the things you've seen, heard of, or imagined – either here or in other organizations – that really work well.

Do you have any questions? *(Respond, then begin.)*

Opening

1. Tell me about a peak experience or high point in your professional life – a time when you felt most alive, most engaged, or really proud of yourself or your work. What was it about you, the situation, the organization, and the leadership that allowed that peak experience to emerge?

2. Tell me about your beginnings with _____ *(name of organization)*.

   - What most attracted you to work here in the first place?

   - Once you were hired, what were the initial impressions that made you proud of the organization?

- Describe one of your earliest positive experiences with the organization, and how that reinforced your initial sense that this was a great place to work.

3. Think of a time when this organization was at its absolute best... when our stakeholders (employees, customers, suppliers, and community members) easily saw who we really are and what we're really about. Tell me about it.

Topic Question(s)

Insert the 3–5 questions that you selected from the Encyclopedia of Positive Questions or created yourself. Be sure to include topics, lead-ins and sub-questions.

Question 1 _____

Topic:

Lead-in:

Sub Questions:

Question 2 _____

<u>**Topic:**</u>

<u>**Lead-in:**</u>

<u>**Sub Questions:**</u>

Question 3 _____

Topic:

Lead-in:

Sub Questions:

Question 4 _____

<u>**Topic:**</u>

<u>**Lead-in:**</u>

<u>**Sub Questions:**</u>

Question 5 _____

Topic:

Lead-in:

Sub Questions:

Closing

1. Imagine you had a magic wand and could have three wishes granted to heighten the health and vitality of this organization. What would they be?

   -
   -
   -

2. What's been the most important thing you've learned – or perhaps re-learned – about _____ (this organization) and yourself, as a result of this conversation we've just shared?

Thanks so much for taking the time to share your thoughts and feelings with me. I've learned a lot about you, this organization, and our possibilities for the future, as a result of this conversation.

In order for us to make full use of all your thoughts and ideas, we'll need to talk over some of the details of what you've shared. I'm guessing this won't be a big deal for you, since the things you've shared are examples of _____ (name of organization) and other organizations at their best.

Still, I want to be sure that I'm representing you in a way that you're comfortable with. So I'd like to ask you to take a few minutes to read over my notes. Let me know if I've

misunderstood anything you've said, or written it in a way that feels uncomfortable for you. Also, let me know if there's anything in those notes that you're unwilling to have quoted or attributed to you, in a public setting.

(either read or let them read notes . . .)

So again, thanks for your time. This conversation has been really interesting for me – and it will help me work with my group to make _____ *(name of organization)* the best it can possibly be.

INTERVIEW SUMMARY SHEET

*(To be completed **within 2 hours** of the end of an interview.)*

1. What were the best stories / quotes that you heard about
   _____ *(name of organization)* in this interview?

2. What were the best stories / quotes that you heard about other
   organizations in this interview?

3. What do these stories and quotes teach us about _____
   (name of organization) at its best?

4. What was the most inspiring dream you heard in this interview?

5. Every now and then, appreciative interviews allow people to dream of ways that their jobs and organizations would be made radically better or more rewarding. If this interview yielded anything along those lines, what was it?

6. What questions about _____ *(name of organization)* does this interview inspire you to want to ask — if any?

Encyclopedia of Positive Questions

INTERVIEW GUIDE

Your Name: _____

Interviewee's Name: _____

Date: _____

Introduction

Thanks for joining me today, and for agreeing to be interviewed
as part of the _____ *(name of
organization or team)* inquiry. Before we get started, let me
take a minute to share with you what we're doing in this
interview, and why we're doing it.

*Insert textual description of what the inquiry is about, why, for
whom, timelines, etc.*

_____

_____

_____

_____

_____

_____

Between _____ and _____, we are conducting interviews with
_____ *(list the people being
interviewed; e.g., employees, customers, suppliers, and
community members)*. We are interviewing people from other
organizations that have a great reputation. We want to learn
about what they do best and how they do it. We want to know

what works best, because we want to find ways to organize around the things that really work, both here and elsewhere.

The questions I'm about to ask you are called appreciative questions. I am going to ask you about times when you have seen things working at their best, both in this organization and in other organizations you've known. Many times we try to ask about things that aren't working well – the problems – so that we can fix them. In this case, we try to find out about the things that are working – the successes – so that we do more of it.

So the best thing you can-do for me in this conversation is to think about, remember, and tell me details about the things you've seen, heard of, or imagined – either here or in other organizations – that really work well.

Do you have any questions? *(Respond, then begin.)*

Opening

1. Tell me about a peak experience or high point in your professional life – a time when you felt most alive, most engaged, or really proud of yourself or your work. What was it about you, the situation, the organization, and the leadership that allowed that peak experience to emerge?

2. Tell me about your beginnings with _____ *(name of organization)*.

   • What most attracted you to work here in the first place?

   • Once you were hired, what were the initial impressions that made you proud of the organization?

- Describe one of your earliest positive experiences with the organization, and how that reinforced your initial sense that this was a great place to work.

3. Think of a time when this organization was at its absolute best... when our stakeholders (employees, customers, suppliers, and community members) easily saw who we really are and what we're really about. Tell me about it.

Topic Question(s)

Insert the 3–5 questions that you selected from the Encyclopedia of Positive Questions or created yourself. Be sure to include topics, lead-ins and sub-questions.

Question 1 _____

Topic:

Lead-in:

Sub Questions:

Question 2 _____

Topic:

Lead-in:

Sub Questions:

Question 3 _____

Topic:

Lead-in:

Sub Questions:

Question 4 _____

Topic:

Lead-in:

Sub Questions:

Question 5 _____

Topic:

Lead-in:

Sub Questions:

Closing

1. Imagine you had a magic wand and could have three wishes granted to heighten the health and vitality of this organization. What would they be?

    •

    •

    •

2. What's been the most important thing you've learned – or perhaps re-learned – about _____ *(this organization)* and yourself, as a result of this conversation we've just shared?

Thanks so much for taking the time to share your thoughts and feelings with me. I've learned a lot about you, this organization, and our possibilities for the future, as a result of this conversation.

In order for us to make full use of all your thoughts and ideas, we'll need to talk over some of the details of what you've shared. I'm guessing this won't be a big deal for you, since the things you've shared are examples of _____ *(name of organization)* and other organizations at their best.

Still, I want to be sure that I'm representing you in a way that you're comfortable with. So I'd like to ask you to take a few minutes to read over my notes. Let me know if I've

misunderstood anything you've said, or written it in a way that feels uncomfortable for you. Also, let me know if there's anything in those notes that you're unwilling to have quoted or attributed to you, in a public setting.

(either read or let them read notes . . .)

So again, thanks for your time. This conversation has been really interesting for me – and it will help me work with my group to make _____ *(name of organization)* the best it can possibly be.

INTERVIEW SUMMARY SHEET

*(To be completed **within 2 hours** of the end of an interview.)*

1. What were the best stories / quotes that you heard about
    _____ *(name of organization)* in this interview?

2. What were the best stories / quotes that you heard about
    other organizations in this interview?

3. What do these stories and quotes teach us about _____
    (name of organization) at its best?

4. What was the most inspiring dream you heard in this interview?

5. Every now and then, appreciative interviews allow people to dream of ways that their jobs and organizations would be made radically better or more rewarding. If this interview yielded anything along those lines, what was it?

6. What questions about _____ *(name of organization)* does this interview inspire you to want to ask – if any?

Encyclopedia of Positive Questions

INTERVIEW GUIDE

Your Name: _____

Interviewee's Name:_____

Date:_____

Introduction

Thanks for joining me today, and for agreeing to be interviewed as part of the _____ *(name of organization or team)* inquiry. Before we get started, let me take a minute to share with you what we're doing in this interview, and why we're doing it.

Insert textual description of what the inquiry is about, why, for whom, timelines, etc.

_____

_____

_____

_____

_____

_____

Between _____ and _____, we are conducting interviews with _____ *(list the people being interviewed; e.g., employees, customers, suppliers, and community members)*. We are interviewing people from other organizations that have a great reputation. We want to learn about what they do best and how they do it. We want to know

what works best, because we want to find ways to organize around the things that really work, both here and elsewhere.

The questions I'm about to ask you are called appreciative questions. I am going to ask you about times when you have seen things working at their best, both in this organization and in other organizations you've known. Many times we try to ask about things that aren't working well – the problems – so that we can fix them. In this case, we try to find out about the things that are working – the successes – so that we do more of it.

So the best thing you can-do for me in this conversation is to think about, remember, and tell me details about the things you've seen, heard of, or imagined – either here or in other organizations – that really work well.

Do you have any questions? *(Respond, then begin.)*

Opening

2. Tell me about a peak experience or high point in your professional life – a time when you felt most alive, most engaged, or really proud of yourself or your work. What was it about you, the situation, the organization, and the leadership that allowed that peak experience to emerge?

2. Tell me about your beginnings with _____ *(name of organization)*.

    •   What most attracted you to work here in the first place?

    •   Once you were hired, what were the initial impressions that made you proud of the organization?

- Describe one of your earliest positive experiences with the organization, and how that reinforced your initial sense that this was a great place to work.

4. Think of a time when this organization was at its absolute best... when our stakeholders (employees, customers, suppliers, and community members) easily saw who we really are and what we're really about. Tell me about it.

Topic Question(s)

Insert the 3–5 questions that you selected from the Encyclopedia of Positive Questions or created yourself. Be sure to include topics, lead-ins and sub-questions.

Question 1 _____

Topic:

Lead-in:

Sub Questions:

Question 2 _____

Topic:

Lead-in:

Sub Questions:

Question 3 _____

Topic:

Lead-in:

Sub Questions:

Question 4 _____

Topic:

Lead-in:

Sub Questions:

Question 5 _____

Topic:

Lead-in:

Sub Questions:

Closing

1. Imagine you had a magic wand and could have three wishes granted to heighten the health and vitality of this organization. What would they be?

    •

    •

    •

2. What's been the most important thing you've learned – or perhaps re-learned – about _____ *(this organization)* and yourself, as a result of this conversation we've just shared?

Thanks so much for taking the time to share your thoughts and feelings with me. I've learned a lot about you, this organization, and our possibilities for the future, as a result of this conversation.

In order for us to make full use of all your thoughts and ideas, we'll need to talk over some of the details of what you've shared. I'm guessing this won't be a big deal for you, since the things you've shared are examples of _____ *(name of organization)* and other organizations at their best.

Still, I want to be sure that I'm representing you in a way that you're comfortable with. So I'd like to ask you to take a few minutes to read over my notes. Let me know if I've

misunderstood anything you've said, or written it in a way that feels uncomfortable for you. Also, let me know if there's anything in those notes that you're unwilling to have quoted or attributed to you, in a public setting.

(either read or let them read notes . . .)

So again, thanks for your time. This conversation has been really interesting for me – and it will help me work with my group to make _____ *(name of organization)* the best it can possibly be.

INTERVIEW SUMMARY SHEET
*(To be completed **within 2 hours** of the end of an interview.)*

1. What were the best stories / quotes that you heard about
    _____ *(name of organization)* in this interview?

2. What were the best stories / quotes that you heard about
    other organizations in this interview?

3. What do these stories and quotes teach us about _____
    (name of organization) at its best?

4. What was the most inspiring dream you heard in this interview?

5. Every now and then, appreciative interviews allow people to dream of ways that their jobs and organizations would be made radically better or more rewarding. If this interview yielded anything along those lines, what was it?

6. What questions about _____ *(name of organization)* does this interview inspire you to want to ask – if any?

Encyclopedia of Positive Questions

INTERVIEW GUIDE

Your Name: _____

Interviewee's Name: _____

Date: _____

Introduction

Thanks for joining me today, and for agreeing to be interviewed as part of the _____ *(name of organization or team)* inquiry. Before we get started, let me take a minute to share with you what we're doing in this interview, and why we're doing it.

Insert textual description of what the inquiry is about, why, for whom, timelines, etc.

_____

_____

_____

_____

_____

_____

Between _____ and _____, we are conducting interviews with _____ *(list the people being interviewed; e.g., employees, customers, suppliers, and community members)*. We are interviewing people from other organizations that have a great reputation. We want to learn about what they do best and how they do it. We want to know

what works best, because we want to find ways to organize around the things that really work, both here and elsewhere.

The questions I'm about to ask you are called appreciative questions. I am going to ask you about times when you have seen things working at their best, both in this organization and in other organizations you've known. Many times we try to ask about things that aren't working well – the problems – so that we can fix them. In this case, we try to find out about the things that are working – the successes – so that we do more of it.

So the best thing you can-do for me in this conversation is to think about, remember, and tell me details about the things you've seen, heard of, or imagined – either here or in other organizations – that really work well.

Do you have any questions? *(Respond, then begin.)*

Opening

3. Tell me about a peak experience or high point in your professional life – a time when you felt most alive, most engaged, or really proud of yourself or your work. What was it about you, the situation, the organization, and the leadership that allowed that peak experience to emerge?

2. Tell me about your beginnings with _____ *(name of organization)*.

   • What most attracted you to work here in the first place?

   • Once you were hired, what were the initial impressions that made you proud of the organization?

- Describe one of your earliest positive experiences with the organization, and how that reinforced your initial sense that this was a great place to work.

5. Think of a time when this organization was at its absolute best... when our stakeholders (employees, customers, suppliers, and community members) easily saw who we really are and what we're really about. Tell me about it.

Topic Question(s)

Insert the 3–5 questions that you selected from the Encyclopedia of Positive Questions or created yourself. Be sure to include topics, lead-ins and sub-questions.

Question 1 _____

Topic:

Lead-in:

Sub Questions:

Question 2 _____

Topic:

Lead-in:

Sub Questions:

Question 3 _____

Topic:

Lead-in:

Sub Questions:

Question 4 _____

Topic:

Lead-in:

Sub Questions:

Question 5 _____

Topic:

Lead-in:

Sub Questions:

Closing

1. Imagine you had a magic wand and could have three wishes granted to heighten the health and vitality of this organization. What would they be?

    •

    •

    •

2. What's been the most important thing you've learned – or perhaps re-learned – about _____ *(this organization)* and yourself, as a result of this conversation we've just shared?

Thanks so much for taking the time to share your thoughts and feelings with me. I've learned a lot about you, this organization, and our possibilities for the future, as a result of this conversation.

In order for us to make full use of all your thoughts and ideas, we'll need to talk over some of the details of what you've shared. I'm guessing this won't be a big deal for you, since the things you've shared are examples of _____ *(name of organization)* and other organizations at their best.

Still, I want to be sure that I'm representing you in a way that you're comfortable with. So I'd like to ask you to take a few minutes to read over my notes. Let me know if I've

misunderstood anything you've said, or written it in a way that feels uncomfortable for you. Also, let me know if there's anything in those notes that you're unwilling to have quoted or attributed to you, in a public setting.

(either read or let them read notes . . .)

So again, thanks for your time. This conversation has been really interesting for me – and it will help me work with my group to make _____ *(name of organization)* the best it can possibly be.

INTERVIEW SUMMARY SHEET

*(To be completed **within 2 hours** of the end of an interview.)*

1. What were the best stories / quotes that you heard about
    _____ *(name of organization)* in this interview?

2. What were the best stories / quotes that you heard about
    other organizations in this interview?

3. What do these stories and quotes teach us about _____
    (name of organization) at its best?

4. What was the most inspiring dream you heard in this interview?

5. Every now and then, appreciative interviews allow people to dream of ways that their jobs and organizations would be made radically better or more rewarding. If this interview yielded anything along those lines, what was it?

6. What questions about _____ (name of organization) does this interview inspire you to want to ask – if any?

Encyclopedia of Positive Questions

Conclusion

The questions in this book provide you with an opportunity to create positive change in your organization. By selecting questions from this booklet and using them to interview colleagues, customers, clients, supervisors, or suppliers, you can renew the sense of positive potential within your organization. People come alive when asked to tell stories of their successes and peak experiences. They enjoy recalling the good times and what they learned. Over and over again, people tell us what a great gift it is to be interviewed, to be listened to for an uninterrupted period of time and to have another person truly interested in them. You can give this gift to your organization.

Remember: the questions we ask are fateful. They set the course for our conversations, which then become our agenda for action. This book is full of questions designed to enhance the capacity of your organization – to set an agenda for organizational success in the topic areas selected. The topics are relevant to any group within the organization. Be sure to select topics that appeal to you. Appreciative Inquiry provides the opportunity to inquire into topics that you and other people in your organization are truly curious about. It is a chance to move beyond cliched business language and to learn from the actual experiences of the people you work with. Choose topics and questions which reflect what you want more of in your organization.

The variety of questions used in Appreciative Inquiry continues to grow. The questions which produce the best and longest lasting change are the ones that are fundamentally affirmative, that include a "half-full" assumption that good things are happening in the organization. The questions in this book are varied. What they share in common is an affirmation that the people in your organization have successful experiences to draw upon and, given a chance, they will enjoy telling their stories and learning from each other. Experiment with the questions, adapt them and arrange them to meet your needs.

How will you know it is working? As you do interviews using the questions in this book we hope that you will experience a renewed sense of enthusiasm and commitment; that you will learn a great deal about working effectively with your colleagues and customers; and that you will enhance relationships with the people you interview. In addition, we hope your interviews ignite a sense of storytelling that brings the best of people and their work to life.

We hope you will be able to generate helpful and fresh interpretations of company dialogues and stories. Sometimes we discover things we are actually proud of in things that we thought we were ashamed of. Sometimes we discover ways of doing things that we thought were impossible. Sometimes we discover that all we have to do is ask and people will tell us the most amazing things – about how to get the job done best.

We also hope that these questions will help you build and strengthen relationships. One AI practitioner, an avid basketball player, says that after a day in which he has played some of his best basketball, he wants to play again with the same people – team mates or opponents. They know what he can-do, and will trust in his abilities. We want to be around people who know us at our best. Using these questions and doing appreciative interviews will help you get to know your colleagues at their best – and give you good reasons to team up with them in the future.

Over the many years that we've used this process in

organizations, we've heard people report three things about their experiences with Appreciative Inquiry. First, it requires a change of habit on their part. Appreciative Inquiry is an invitation to positive thinking, listening, and talking. It is a form of positive change.

Most people start out wondering if what they are going to hear will be useful; and they end up being amazed by what they learn and the relationships they make using Appreciative Inquiry. For many people it requires a change of habit but not a change of heart. Second, people feel energized by conducting interviews. They report feeling inspired, motivated, and in awe. They gain respect for colleagues and customers and they want to do more to help them succeed. They learn more in one interview than in hours of meetings. Third, people report experiences of spontaneity, creativity and innovation. Interviews help groups of people think "out of the box" as they discover new ideas and possibilities in the stories of past highpoints and future dreams. In short, appreciative interviews can be rewarding in special and surprising ways. We hope that you and your colleagues truly enjoy them.

This book suggests ten ways to share Appreciative Inquiry stories and information. We offer these ideas as starting points. Like everything else in the book, adapt them to meet your needs. The capacity to generate information, and share it across an organization can be a strategic advantage. Recognition of success creates a positive work environment, which can also be a strategic advantage. Find ways to share the stories you hear when you do interviews. Be creative and create new ways to spread good news, celebrate successes and share information across the organization.

We have seen Appreciative Inquiry help people and their

organizations on many levels – personally, strategically, financially and emotionally. We believe it can help make our world a better place. We welcome you to share in this hope.

Lakeshore Publications in Appreciative Inquiry: 2001-2002

ISBN	Author(s)	Title	Price	X Quantity	= Total
1893435334	Whitney/Cooperrider/et al	Ency. Pos. Questions	15.95	_____	$_____
1893435342	Cooperrider	AI: The Beginnings	62.00	_____	$_____
1893435172	Cooperrider/Whitney	AI Handbook (w/CD)	59.00	_____	$_____
1893435385	Cooperrider/Whitney	AI Handbook (Only)	32.00	_____	$_____
1893435059	Srivastva/Coop.	Appreciative Mgmt.	49.00	_____	$_____
1893435423	Mahe/Gibbs	Giving Birth New Org.	18.95	_____	$_____

SUBTOTAL: $_____

SHIPPING: add $3.00 plus 8% of Subtotal $_____

TOTAL: $_____

Name: _____

Institution Name:_____

Address: _____

City: _____ State: _____ Zip: _____

Telephone: (_____) _____

E-Mail: _____

Librarians Note: For Single copy sales, PREPAYMENT IS REQUIRED. Checks made payable to Lakeshore Communications or Credit Card Payment must accompany order.

Our distributors are:
Baker & Taylor, Blackwells, and Ingrams.

 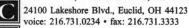

LAKESHORE COMMUNICATIONS
PRINTING, PUBLISHING, AND MULTIMEDIA
24100 Lakeshore Blvd., Euclid, OH 44123
voice: 216.731.0234 • fax: 216.731.3333
email: cservice1@lakeshorepublishers.com
www.lakeshorepublishers.com

LAKESHORE COMMUNICATIONS:
THE "APPRECIATIVE INQUIRY" PUBLISHER

Published:

- Srivastva, S., and Cooperrider, D.: Appreciative Management and Leadership   (1999)
  ISBN: 1893435-059 $49.00   548pp

Spring 2002 Publications:

- Cooperrider, D. and Whitney, D.; Appreciative Inquiry Handbook
  ISBN: 1893435-172 $59.00   280pp   6-15-2002

  A handbook which combines theory with practice, aimed at Consultants, Trainers, and leaders of Organizational Change. The handbook (with accompanying software and a Web site offering "modular" download capability) aims to help trainers: a.) Understand the Foundations of Appreciative Inquiry; b.) Appreciate the wide range of applications for Appreciative Inquiry; c.) Facilitate the teaching/coaching of others in introducing Appreciative Inquiry to a new group. Thus, tools and activities are included as PowerPoint applications, to facilitate group teaching and dissemination.

- Mahe, S., and Gibbs, C.: Giving Birth to A New Organization
  "United Religions Initiative Meets Appreciative Inquiry"
  ISBN: 1893435-423 $18.95   280pp   6-15-2002

  The birth of the United Religions Initiative (URI) is the story of how hundreds, then thousands of people across cultures, oceans, and faith traditions began to share a common call to make the world they lived in more like the world they yearned for in their dreams. This book tells how one person's vision and conviction evolved to include a global community working together to make their dreams real – dreams reflected in a call of the sacred within a worldwide, faith-based organization.

  The book also tells the story of how an emergent process of organizational change – the Appreciative Inquiry (AI) process – came along at just the right time to serve as a midwife for the new organization and its development. AI, its practitioners and its process, provided the values and the practical guidance that gave birth to a locally rooted, globally connected organization which would be: inclusive, decentralized and self-organizing. AI and the URI together embarked upon a "spiritual journey"; the theme of this narrative.

More Information @ www.lakeshorepublishers.com